Amazing Pictures and Facts About Iran

By: Mina Kelly

Introduction

Susa, one of Iran's first cities was developed in the year 3200 B.C. This makes Iran one of the oldest nations in the world! Iran has been a source of great history, as millions of people have lived there and passed through the country. Let's explore the wonders of Iran!

What is the Official Name of Iran?

Iran is officially called Jomhuri-ye Eslami-ye Iran. In short
form, it is written as Iran.

What is the Geography Like in Iran?

Iran's geography is very mountainous. The country also has desert lands that run almost 800 miles long!

Where is Iran Located?

Iran is located in Asia. Iran is bordered by Turkey, Azerbaijan, Armenia, Afghanistan, Pakistan and Turkmenistan.

How Big is Iran?

Iran is 636,293 square miles in area. Iran is the 18th largest country in the world by size.

What is the Climate Like in Iran?

Iran's climate is categorized as subtropical. The weather is usually quite hot, with long summers and short winters.

Are There Unique Animals in Iran?

There are many small mice such as the Avicenna field mouse and the Iranian shrew that are native to the country. Iran is also home to the Asiatic cheetah, a subspecies that is slowly dying out.

What is the Flag of Iran Like?

The flag of Iran has three horizontal stripes that are equal in size. The top is green, the middle is white and the bottom is red. The center symbol features a sword that symbolized the strength of the country and the five principles of Islam.

What is the Capital of Iran Called?

The capital of Iran is called Tehran. Tehran is also the largest city in the country.

How Many People Live in Iran?

Iran is home to a whopping 80 million people! It is estimated that 73% of that population live in an urban area.

What is the Currency of Iran?

The currency of Iran is called the Iranian rial. The currency code for the Iranian rial is written as IRR.

What is the Highest Peak of Iran Called?

The highest peak in Iran is called Mount Damavand. Mount Damavand is 18,406 feet tall!

What do People Eat in Iran?

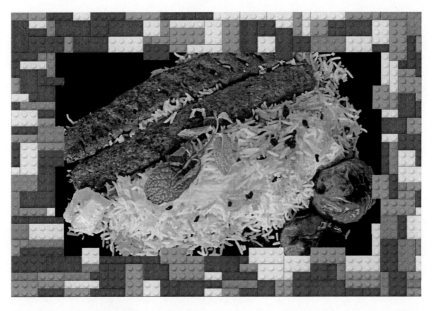

Fesenjan, better known as pomegranate walnut stew is a popular dish for main events in Iran. Rice is also cooked often, as it can be prepared with a variety of spices and meats.

What is the Government of Iran Called?

The government of Iran is a Theocratic Islamic Republic. The officials are appointed, rather than elected. The supreme leader is usually appointed for life.

What is the Main Religion in Iran?

Islam is the most popular religion practiced in Iran. The two most practiced branches of Islam in Iran are Sunni and Shi'i.

What are the Main Exports of Iran?

The main exports of Iran include oils and other natural gases, fruits, metals and plastics. Iran exports its goods to places like China, Japan and Turkey.

What is the Most Popular Sport in Iran?

Wrestling and football (Soccer) are popular sports in Iran. Interestingly, it is estimated that only 20% of the Iranian population is physically active.

What Types of Plants and Trees are in Iran?

In the mountains wild fruit such as pears, pomegranates and walnuts grow on trees. The elevation within the mountains dictates what grows, because plants need a healthy water source.

What is the Average Life Expectancy of the Iranian People?

The Iranian men live to be 71 years on average, while the women live to be 74 years old on average. Do you know how long women and men live to be in your country?

What is the Official Language of Iran?

Persian is the official language of Iran. Persian may also be referred to as Farsi.

What is the Longest River in Iran Called?

The longest river that passes through Iran is called the Aras river. The longest river that is only within the borders of Iran is called the Karun River.

Made in the USA
San Bernardino, CA
08 November 2017